# L-ISTORJA TAN-NUMRI

## THE NUMBER STORY

### SMALL BOOK ONE

#### ENGLISH - MALTESE

*Numbers Teach Children*
*Their Number Names*

*written and illustrated by*

## MISS ANNA

Early Reader Edition of *The Number Story 1*
Bronze Medal Winner, 2016 Wishing Shelf Book Award

Library of Congress Control Number: 2018902040

Names: Miss Anna, author.
Title: Number story : numbers teach children their number names / Miss Anna.
Description: Portland, OR: Lumpy Publishing, 2018.
Identifiers: ISBN 978-1-945977-45-9 | LCCN 2018902040
Summary: The pictures and rhymes present stories which introduce numbers 0-10.
Subjects: LCSH Numeration—English--Macedonian--Pictorial works--Juvenile literature. | BISAC JUVENILE NONFICTION /
Languages: English--Macedonian
Classification: LCC QA141.3 .M57 2018 | DDC 513—dc23

Publisher: Lumpy Publishing
Website: www.missannabooks.com
Email: missanna@missannabooks.com

Paperback: ISBN 978-1-945977-45-9
Printed in the U.S.A.    1 3 5 7 9 10 8 6 4 2

Сакаш да ги научиш имињата на броевите?

It is very easy and a lot of fun!

Лесно е и забавно!

Say-along our little jingle

Пејте заедно со нас.

starting from Number One!

**Nibdew min-numru wieħed!**

1

ONE     looks like my one finger.

WIEĦED

Jidher bħal saba tiegħi.

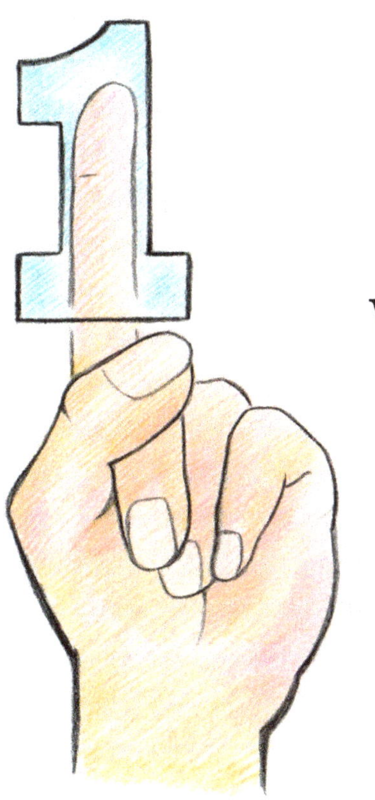

ONE!
WIEĦED!

# 2

TWO trails a tail.

TNEJN

għandu denb.

A TAIL!  DENB!

# 3

THREE has bumps.

## TLIETA

huwa bħal għoljiet.

BUMPY! GHOLJIET!

# 4

FOUR  carries a sail.

ERBGĦA

huwa dgħajsa tal-qlugħ.

A SAIL!
QLUGH!

5

FIVE   is a racing track.

ĦAMSA

huwa trek tat-tiġrija.

VROOM
VROOOM!

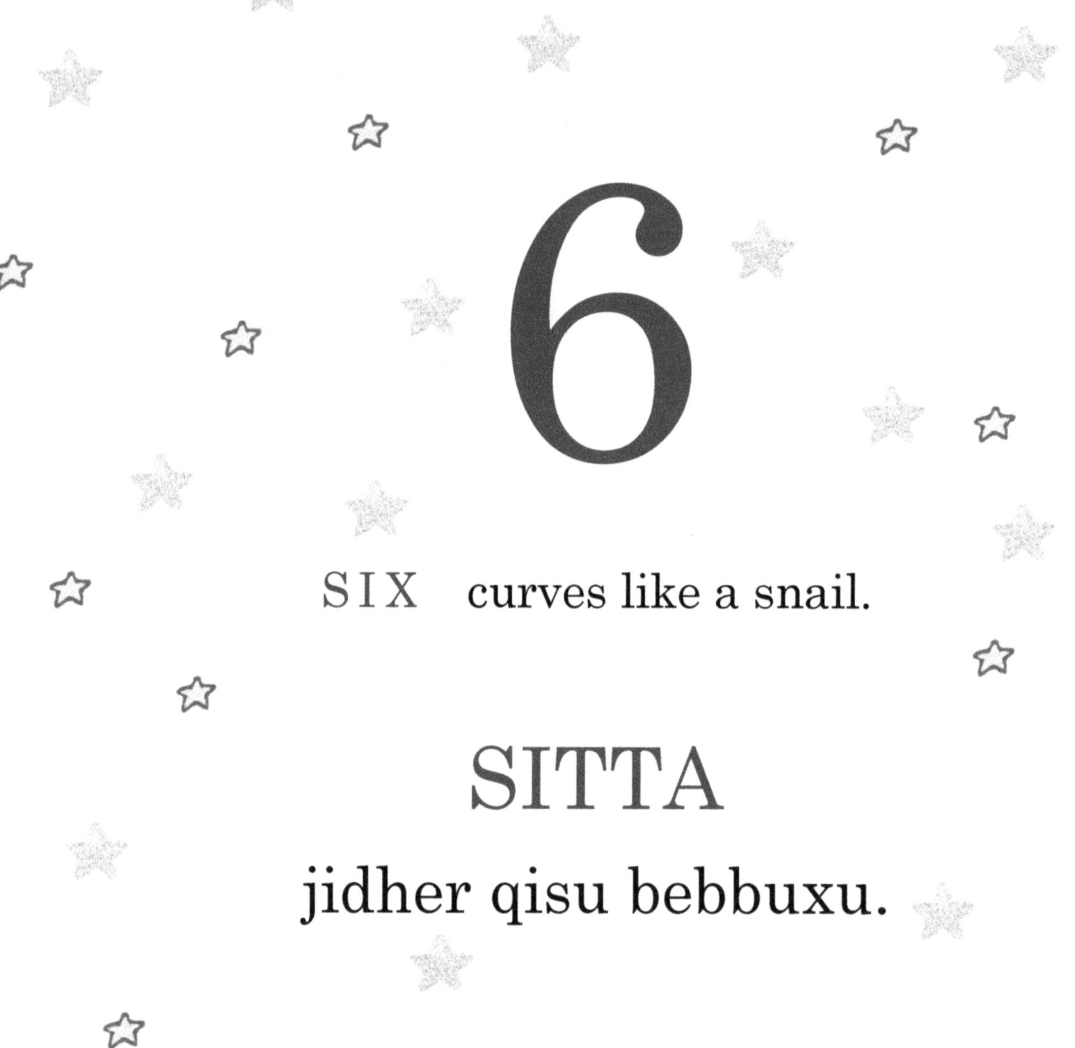

# 6

SIX curves like a snail.

SITTA

jidher qisu bebbuxu.

A SNAIL!  BEBBUXU!

7

OUCH!
OUCH!

# 8

E I G H T   is rollercoaster rails.

## TMIENJA

huwa bħal *rollercoaster*.

YIPPEE!

YIPPEE!

NINE   is a bubble on a stick.

DISGĦA

huwa bużżieqa fuq stikka.

# A BUBBLE! BUZZIEQA!

# 10

TEN   is an eye of a whale.

GĦAXRA

huwa għajn ta' baliena.

HELLO!
HELOW!

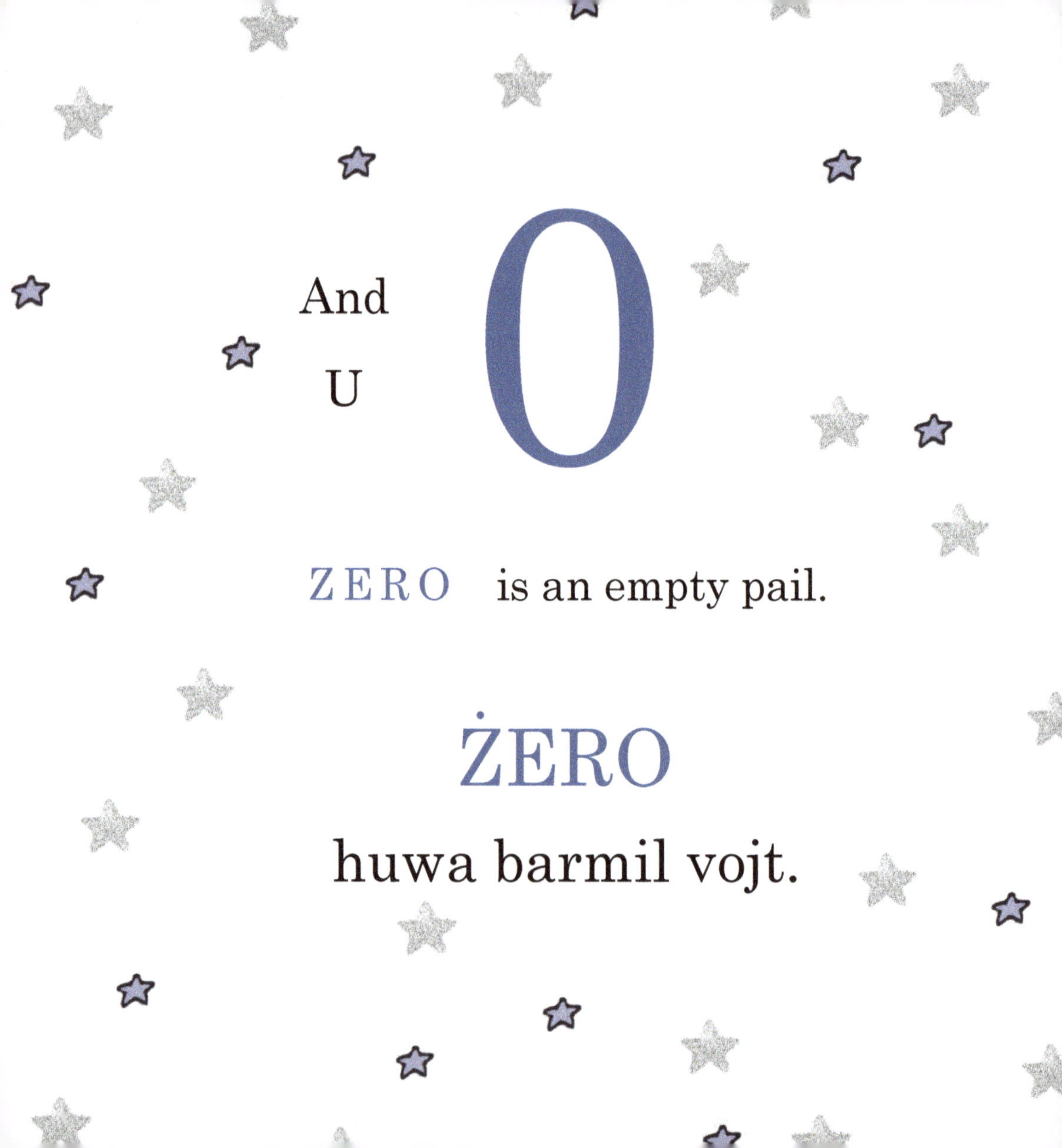
And
U

O

ZERO   is an empty pail.

ŻERO

huwa barmil vojt.

IT'S
EMPTY!
VOJT!

Thank you for playing with us today.

We had a lot of fun too!

Grazzi talli lgħabtu magħna llum.

Aħna ħadna gost ukoll!

We are your Number friends,
Zero to Ten,
Who will be here for you~
Aħna l-ħbieb tiegħek
Żero sa Għaxra.
Se nkunu hawn għalik~


Bye-bye now!
See you again soon!
Saħħa issa!
Nerġgħu narawk ma ndumux!

The Numbers are *SINGING* too!

To sing-a-long, look for Miss Anna Number Story
at your favorite music store like iTUNES.

MP3

## Numbers 0-10
IDENTIFYING
& COUNTING

## Numbers 11-20
& Ordinals

first, second, third...

## Numbers 0-100
& Place Values

ones, tens, hundreds...

## About Clocks
& Telling Time

hours, minutes, seconds...

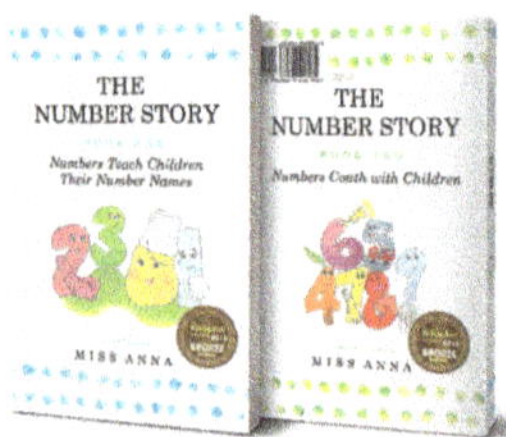

Number Story 1 & 2

isbn: 978-0-996216-48-7

Number Story 3 & 4

isbn: 978-1-945977-01-5

Number Story 5 & 6

isbn: 978-1-945977-06-0

Number Story 7 & 8

isbn: 978-1-949320-40-4

For more Miss Anna books to love,
visit us at

www.missannabooks.com

Numbers are working hard all over the world!
*Come Travel the World with Us!*

www.ingramcontent.com/pod-product-compliance
Lightning Source LLC
Chambersburg PA
CBHW041100050726

47599CB00018B/2219